The Overnight Guide to

DRESSING

THIN

by Mary Martin Niepold

RUNNING PRESS
Philadelphia, Pennsylvania

Copyright ©1986 by
Running Press.

Printed in the United States. All rights
reserved under the Pan-American and
International Copyright Conventions.

*This book may not be reproduced in
whole or in part in any form or by any
means, electronic or mechanical, including photocopying, recording, or by
any information storage and retrieval
system now known or hereafter invented,
without written permission from the
publisher.*

Library of Congress Cataloging in
Publication Data:
  Niepold, Mary Martin.
    Dressing thin.

    1. Clothing and dress. 2. Beauty,
Personal.
I. Title.
TT507.N47 1986   646'.34   86–10202
ISBN 0-89471-456-2 (pbk.)
ISBN 0-89471-457-0 (lib. bdg.)

Canadian representatives: General
Publishing Co., Ltd., 30 Lesmill Road,
Don Mills, Ontario M3B 2T6.

9 8 7 6 5 4 3 2 1

Digit on the right indicates the number
of this printing.

Cover design by Toby Schmidt
Photography by Christophe von
  Hohenberg
Styling by Mary Martin Niepold
Makeup and hairstyling by Chris
  Welles
Models: Jody Alaimo, Christine Feezel,
  Barbara Fimbel, Susan Schwirck
Printed by Command Web,
  Secaucus, NJ
Typography: Garth Graphic by rci,
  Philadelphia, PA

This book may be ordered from the
publisher. Please include $1.00 for
postage. *But try your bookstore first!*
Running Press Book Publishers
125 South 22nd Street
Philadelphia, Pennsylvania 19103

Credits

Page 45: Suit by Albert Nipon; hat
by Makins

Page 46: Wool knit two-piece dress
by Peter Lynne; large gold
earrings by Francine
Harris

Page 47: Jacket and blouse by
Givenchy en Plus; pin by
Francine Harris

Page 50: Jacket and skirt by
Jocelyn of Paris

Page 51: Suit and tank blouse by
Jocelyn of Paris;
stone/chain drop earrings
by Francine Harris

Page 52: Straight black georgette
skirt by Judith Ann

Page 54: Dress by Givenchy en
Plus

Page 55: Dress by Albert Nipon;
long, dangling white
earrings by Francine
Harris

Page 56: Dress by Albert Nipon

Page 57: Lightweight wool dress by
Rothschild; abstract silver
and jewel pin by Francine
Harris

Page 58: "Cool wool" mustard coat
by Rothschild; black felt
hat by Makins; pin by
Francine Harris

Page 59: Beaded gown by Judith
Ann; earrings by Francine
Harris

Page 60: Hat by Makins

Page 61: Beaded dress by Judith
Ann

Page 63: Floral bigshirt by Ricky
Smithline

Page 64: Cotton jersey jumpsuit by
Ricky Smithline

Page 70: Black felt hat by Makins;
long rope of silver and
beads by Francine Harris

Contents

Introduction

Come on, tell the truth: your body isn't such a bad thing, is it?

Sure, those extra pounds or bulges may make you wish for cheerleader practice and those days when you didn't even have to think about anything extra—but those 10 or 20 pounds are there, and the worst thing you can do is to let them fill your life with endless sighs of displeasure with yourself. Extra pounds don't make you less lovable.

If, however, agonizing about extra pounds makes you feel less than yourself, there's another way to feel: it's called "liking what I've got until I get what I really want." The secret? Capitalize on what you *do* have.

The right clothes will make you look thinner and let you feel a lot better until you lose (or even if you don't lose) those extra pounds.

The art of dressing thin is no more or less than recognizing your assets, dressing to show off your good parts, minimizing the extra parts—and always grinning at that new, thinner version of yourself.

It's really very simple: fashion is the art of illusion, and the right clothes can actually make you look thinner, whatever your size. A burst of color here, a drape of fabric there—even big, dazzling jewelry can help you look 10 or 20 pounds lighter.

The right fashions become your ally, not your adversary, when you know which ones are best for you.

You don't necessarily have to diet to achieve a look other people would "die for"; throw out that lettuce and lemon juice. Learn, instead, what parts of your body to accent and what parts to de-emphasize.

Your body, whatever its size, is the best thing you've got going for you. Unless you weigh in at 30 or 40 pounds more than what's good for you, you've got good, visible attributes worth emphasizing. Almost no one gains weight evenly. So, strut those thin ankles; expose those sensuous arms; let the world see that languid neck; wrap that well-defined waist in electric colors! Show off whatever it is that's good, extra pounds notwithstanding.

The Dressing Thin Formula is this: maximize the good, and minimize the extra.

Welcome to the world of illusion—and to feeling better about yourself.

1 How to Analyze Your Body

The first step to dressing thin is to step into a leotard or nothing at all. Don't fudge with a swimsuit that pulls you in or a bra that lifts you up. Now, stand in front of a full-length mirror, and look.

In this age when most people still believe that "you can never be too rich or too thin," as the Duchess of Windsor suggested years ago, smile as you look at your whole body in the mirror. That full-length mirror is the first step to looking thin and enjoying it—acknowledging where you are heavy and where your good attributes are.

The mirror has to be full-length. There's no other accurate way for you to figure out what you've got and what most needs camouflaging.

So, buy that mirror, stand in front of a friend's, or visit a department store at a time when it's relatively empty and you can strip down to your bare essentials in semi-privacy.

The best choice is to have your very own full-length mirror; as a matter of fact, owning one could be one of the best investments you'll ever make. Whether you're overweight or just right, you can count on that mirror to show you what you really look like. It also will help you get an accurate overall picture of yourself when you're dressed: it will show you proportion, color, symmetry—that head-to-toe image that everyone else sees.

Standing there in all your natural glory may be the hardest part of dressing thin, but it's the most important part. Take a deep breath—and a good look.

STEP 1: Your Basic Body Type

First, look at your body head to toe—front, back, and sideways. Have a friend look, too, if you can. Someone else's view of you is a good assurance that you're not kidding yourself when you start recording the parts of your body.

What you're looking for, and what you will write down, are the beautiful parts—worth emphasizing— and the bumps and bulges—worth de-emphasizing. You will record your measurements, up and down as well as all around.

There are several basic body types, and yours, generally, is going to match one of them.

Anthropologists tell us there are three body shapes: ectomorph, mesomorph, and endomorph. The ectomorph is the small-framed person with almost no visible muscle or fat, some shaping in the bust, usually narrow shoulders, and hips more narrow than shoulders. The mesomorph has a medium build: there's more visible muscle and bone, but not much fat; shoulders can be broad, and there's some narrowness in the rib cage, waist, and hips. The endomorph has a heavy build, usually rounded on all sides, with a thick middle section. There's really not much excess fat, muscles are firm, and shoulders frequently are narrower than hips.

In truth, each of us fits one of these basic body types, but since we all gain weight in different areas

of our bodies, four basic shapes emerge. Your job
now is to look at your body to see which of these four
types is closest to yours. The four types are:

▶ *Straight up and down.* Similar to a rounded-all-over
or endomorph shape, this body has no defined
waist; shoulders, waist, hips, and thighs are about
the same width.

▶ *Top-heavy.* This body is heavy in the bust. Usually,
hips and thighs appear narrower than bust and
shoulders.

▶ *Bottom-heavy.* Also called pear-shaped, this body is
broad in the beam, with hips and thighs wider than
the shoulders.

▶ *Hourglass.* No matter how many extra pounds it
carries, this body is still blessed with a well-defined
waist.

Look very closely at your full image in the mirror,
front and back, to see where the total *outside* lines of
your body are defined. Imagine that you are looking
at a pencil-drawn silhouette of your body.

A trick that helps determine which of these four
body types is yours is something called "the squint."
Fashion designers and stylists often use this trick to
get a view of the total silhouette of clothes, as well as
a head-to-toe image of the "whole" look when dressing models for photos or runway shows. Art students
do the same thing: I've watched my son, a student in
a fine arts college, squint whenever he's sketching
figures. For some reason, when we look through half-
mast eyes, extraneous details are minimized and a
reliable, fluid line of the whole body emerges.

Record your body type. Now it's time to get out a
tape measure and take measurements that will verify
your type.

Of course, these are the numbers that give you the
jitters. But the inches you record will be a quick ref-

9

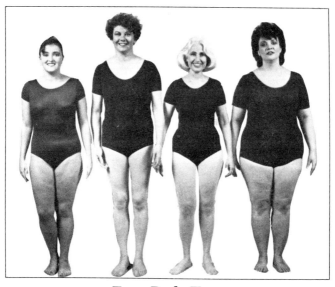

Four Body Types

Straight up and down
(Left)
37–35–39"
Shoulders: 15"
Widest part of thighs: 24½"
Neck to waist (front): 15"
Neck to waist (back): 16½"
Waist to crotch: 11"
Shoulders to crotch: 23"
Crotch to ankles: 23"

Specific areas:
Small, high breasts
Short waist
Thick waist and torso
Protruding derriere
Hips as wide as shoulders
Legs roughly as long as torso

Top-heavy
(Second from left)
42–35–37"
Shoulders: 17½"
Widest part of thighs: 23"
Neck to waist (front): 16"
Neck to waist (back): 19"
Waist to crotch: 13"
Shoulders to crotch: 25½"
Crotch to ankles: 32"

Specific areas:
Large, low breasts
Average-length torso
Average-to-thin torso
Protruding tummy
Flat derriere
*Hips and thighs narrower
    than shoulders*
Long legs

Bottom-heavy
(Second from right)
34½–29–39½"
Shoulders: 14"
Widest part of thighs: 23½"
Neck to waist (front): 14"
Neck to waist (back): 14"
Waist to crotch: 11½"
Shoulders to crotch: 21½"
Crotch to ankles: 30"

Specific areas:
Small, high breasts
Narrow shoulders
Short waist
Saddlebags
Protruding tummy
Protruding derriere
Long legs

Hourglass
(Right)
46–38–49"
Shoulders: 18"
Widest part of thighs: 28½"
Neck to waist (front): 14"
Neck to waist (back): 18"
Waist to crotch: 13½"
Shoulders to crotch: 23½"
Crotch to ankles: 30"

Specific areas:
Ample, high breasts
Shoulders and hips same
  width
Protruding tummy
Torso as long as legs
Average derriere
No saddlebags

erence to your plus and minus areas. At this point, you're not trying to find out how far off the magical 36–24–36 ideal you may be. You're simply recording the truth about your body shape.

STEP 2: Around

Hold the tape measure a bit loosely (don't cheat by pulling it tight) and record these measurements:
▶ *Bust.* Place the tape just under your shoulder blades and pull it around and over the fullest part of your bust.
▶ *Waist.* Imagine where a waistband feels most comfortable on you, place the tape there, and don't take a deep breath when you measure. Gently wrap the tape around your waist; if you come out with a fractional measurement, record that, too. A half-

inch can go a long way in determining what clothes will minimize your figure.

▶ *Hips.* Gather your courage, and place the tape on the fullest part of your hips. For some people, it's the upper part of the hips around the pelvic bones; for others, it's the middle or lower part.

▶ *Shoulders.* Ask someone to stretch the tape measure across your back, from shoulder to shoulder at their widest points.

▶ *Thighs.* Find the widest part of your thighs and measure from these outside widest points. This will tell you whether you have "saddlebags" and where your thighs are widest.

Write down these five measurements under your body type. Does this set of numbers match the overall body silhouette you determined in Step 1? If it doesn't, take another full view of yourself and see if the widths of shoulders, bust, waist, hips, and upper thighs are in line with the above measurements.

STEP 3: Up and Down

Now it's time to record some length measurements. What you're looking for here are certain longitudinal measurements that reflect your head-to-foot body structure. These will give you a more complete analysis of your body type. You'll need a friend to help you with some of these measurements; and again, don't pull the tape too taut.

Measure the distance from:

▶ *Neck to Waist.* To determine whether you are short-waisted, long-waisted, or average, and whether your waist is the same length front and back, take these measurements both in front and back. Not all of us are evenly distributed; your upper torso may be average-length in front, but shorter in back, or vice versa.

Stand with your legs together. In front, measure from the center of your neck, just above your collarbone to the center of your waist, which is usually close to your navel or wherever the tape felt most comfortable when you measured your waist.

Still standing with your legs together, ask someone to measure from just below the base of your neck to the center of your waist in the back. Again, it's the center of that waistline where the tape felt most comfortable around you. Record both measurements, front and back.

▶ *Waist to Crotch.* Measure from that same center part of your waist in front to a point just at the base of your crotch. Record these inches.

Having recorded these three sets of numbers, you now have an idea of the length of your torso and whether it is equally long or short.

To determine if your legs are short or long compared to the rest of your body, measure the following:

▶ *Shoulders to Crotch.* Measure diagonally, from the tops of your shoulders, at their outside edges, to the base of your crotch. Record these measurements.

▶ *Crotch to Ankles.* With your legs still together, measure from the base of your crotch straight down to where your ankles meet. Record this.

Look at these two new sets of measurements. All of these numbers—from neck to waist to crotch to ankles—will pinpoint how your bone structure is aligned length-wise.

If the length from your *neck to waist* is the same length or less than the measurement from your *waist to crotch,* you're probably short-waisted and your legs are proportionately longer than your torso.

If the measurement from your *shoulders to crotch* is roughly three to four inches longer than the measurement from your *crotch to ankles,* you have a long torso, and your legs are shorter than your torso.

Looking at these sets of measurements, you now know whether your torso and your legs are short, long, or average. These facts, along with your basic body type, will determine the kinds of clothes that will best enhance your proportions, as well as masquerade any bulges.

For example, you may be a straight-up-and-down body type, but if you're long-waisted and short-legged as well, certain kinds of clothes can create the illusion of longer legs and a more balanced proportion lengthwise, and de-emphasize those areas where you're thickest.

Knowing these measurements will teach you how to dress to decrease your "extras," and how to choose clothes that help balance your shape, length-wise.

STEP 4: Sideways

By looking at your body sideways, you'll see other shapes you'll need to consider in learning to dress thin.

Stand with your legs together and with your body sideways to the mirror. Look closely at this up-and-down, side view of yourself. Record these shapes:

▶ *Bust.* From the side, does your bust appear small, medium, or ample? Do your breasts hang low or stay close to your chest? Write down both these aspects of your breast configuration. (For example: "medium breasts, erect"; or "full breasts, low.")

▶ *Derriere.* Still looking at the side view of yourself, zero in on how your bottom is shaped. Does it protrude? Is it of average prominence, meaning that it doesn't extend much farther out than the extension of your shoulders as seen from the side? Or do you have virtually no bottom as seen from the side? Record which of these three derriere types you are.

▶ *Stomach.* Still looking at yourself from the side, look at your stomach. Does your tummy bulge frontward from under your waistline? If so, is it a moderate bulge? Or is there no bulge at all? If you've ever seen a woman who looked reed-thin from the front and who then turned sideways and presented the silhouette of a pregnant woman, you understand why a protruding stomach is something you'd rather not have others notice. Write down which tummy type is yours.

Now it's time to stand frontward and backward in front of the mirror. You're looking for other pluses and minuses in your body.

▶ *Arms.* Are the upper portions heavy? If so, are they also heavily shaped from the elbow down? Or is the weight evenly distributed from shoulder to wrist? Record the shape of your arms.

▶ *Thighs.* Boy, is this a trouble area for a lot of women! Well, face up to this truth about your body. Knowing whether thighs are a plus or a minus is vital to knowing which kinds of skirts and jackets best suit you. Look closely at your thighs, from front and back. Do they bulge just under where your hips end? Or are your upper thighs the same width as your hips, or thinner? Record your upper-thigh shape.

▶ *Lower Legs.* Record whether you have thin ankles and well-shaped lower legs or whether the bottom portion of your legs is also heavy, with little ankle definition. Look, also, at the backs of your knees; this definitely can tell you what length of skirt and what kinds of shorts are right for you.

▶ *Waist.* Yes, you've got to look at your waist again. Is it well defined? Is it narrower than your hips? Is it narrower than your shoulders? Is it noticeably narrower than your shoulders *and* your hips?

15

Note your waist indentation: well defined, slightly defined, no definition. This notation will tell you a lot about whether to wear snazzy belts or forget them altogether.

▶ *Neck and Face.* Are your neck and face taut, or are you fleshy in these areas? Is your face chiseled, medium-shaped, or round? Ditto for your neck. It's critical to know these facts about yourself, because in choosing makeup, hairstyles, and jewelry, it's essential to know whether your face and neck need enhancing with a bit of fashion camouflage. Eyes, as they say, are the windows of the soul, and a bright, happy face goes a long way to winning the Battle of Troy—or anything else.

▶ *Shoulders and Back.* For summer dressing or for gala dressy events, it's critical to understand this area of your body. Is the shape of your back and shoulders average, or are you fleshy here? A strapless gown could be your enemy or your fairy godmother, so write down how muscle and flesh are distributed here.

STEP 5: Minus and Plus

Whew—the mirror torture is now over. Recording these cold, analytical facts about yourself is no easy thing, but once you know the inches, lengths, and thicknesses of your body, you're ready to put those facts to work for you.

Remember, none of us gains weight evenly, or in all the same places. None of us has exactly the same body shape, sideways or long-ways. Your body type and your body's pluses and minuses are as unique as your personality. Clothing, at its best, is a way to strut what's good and leave everything else to illusion, or to no notice at all.

By now, you have a pretty extensive list of facts about your body: not only do you know your basic body type, but you also have a wonderful list of your assets. And chances are that if you review those nine specific body areas, you've already learned that you've got some beautiful things going for you— whatever the amount of thickness or number of bulges elsewhere.

Now, take this information and condense it on paper. Record your body shape. Record your bust-waist-hip measurements right beneath it. Next, going through the nine specific body areas, separate what you've learned about your body into plus and minus columns.

For example:

Body Type: Straight up and down

Measurements: 35½–30–36″

Pluses:	Minuses:
Long, thin arms and wrists	*Short waist*
Thighs no wider at the top than hips	*Waist almost as thick as top of hips*
Moderately thin lower legs and ankles	*Waist shorter in back than in front*
Moderately protruding tummy	*Hips thicker at top than middle or lower sections*
Unfleshy shoulders and neck	
Moderately chiseled face	
Long legs	
Bust medium, but erect	

Now go ahead—get it down on paper!

Body Type: _____

Measurements: _____

Pluses: _____   Minuses: _____

Isn't it amazing how many pluses you discovered?

Whether you have more pluses than minuses isn't the issue. The point is that you *do* have pluses—and by understanding what they are, you can begin to maximize the good, minimize the extra. These hard, cold facts about your body are your guide to choosing clothes that will automatically make you look thinner.

One more thing: photocopy this information. An index card should be sufficient; make several copies, and keep one in your wallet for reference when you shop. Tape another copy to the refrigerator door for those times when midnight hedonism seems more important than not wanting to feel like a less-than-perfect plop of porridge. Tape another copy to that full-length mirror, which from this day forward is going to be the second-best set of eyes you could ever wish for.

You might write something else at the bottom of that card:

"I've got a lot going for me, and 20 extra pounds have little to do with it. What I've got is liking myself until, or if ever, I become someone I like better."

Congratulations: the referees just clanged the bell on round one of Dressing Thin, and you're already ahead of the game.

2 The Four Fashion Basics

Before you can understand whether a row of fuchsia orchids looks right or wrong dancing across your particular bust, you need to know some basic principles of fashion design.

Like art, fashion is an assortment of visual elements which make a pretty or not-so-pretty picture when they're combined. In fashion, the four basic elements are pattern, color, shape, and proportion. No matter what your size or weight, or how your weight is distributed, how well you apply these four principles to your own body type will determine how you look.

Once you understand how to use pattern, color, shape, and proportion, you can add these elements to what you already know about your body and come out a fashion winner.

Pattern

One of the most obvious visual impacts is created by either the texture of a fabric or its print. Textured fabrics such as silk jacquards, as well as ribbed and accordion-pleated fabrics, also create the effect of a pattern.

You'll want to avoid adding heavily textured fabrics to any part of your body that's heavy. Mohair and long-haired fur coats will add pounds, and so will ribbed silks and large jacquard fabrics. Even when an overall "pattern" is in one color value, the fabric will still bring attention to that part of the body if the jacquard motif is too large.

Prints can range from the babiest of checks to nuclear-sized cabbage roses. Small prints are safe for all of us—unless they're whipped up in chartreuse and royal blue, electric colors so bright that they, not the pattern, pull attention to the part of the body where they're worn.

Obviously, you'd be stretching your chances for looking thin if you draped wide hips in bionic flowers or stage-sized geometrics, or if you added a wide, multicolored belt to a thick waist, or pulled a sweater with a large pattern over a chest that's already large enough, thank you.

Patterns can work for you if you know how to use them. Vertical stripes are, of course, one of the surest camouflages, and diagonal stripes can create a visual effect that cuts away thick areas. You may be surprised to learn that even horizontal stripes are a possibility—but only for a straight-up-and-down body whose overall weight is not that far from the norm, or for those areas of the body where extra extension is needed, such as the shoulders of a bottom-heavy body.

A key to wearing stripes, horizontal ones included, is their size: awning stripes won't work for anyone who tips the scales a bit.

In choosing *any* pattern—whether stripes, butterflies, or anything else—the size of the pattern is essential. In the case of patterns, less is definitely not more; here, less is a beautiful less.

Color

What would we do without color? It adds gusto, cheeriness, dazzle, and allure. And why shouldn't it add these same effects to an extra 10 pounds of you?

Of all the elements in the fashion mix, color may well be your most important opening shot. It's the first thing other people notice about your outfit, and it tells people how you see yourself. With color, you can subtly flirt or boldly flaunt your best features. If smiles can make you look upbeat and worthy of being looked at, so can colors.

Let's debunk a fashion myth that says that black is only for widows, the wealthy, or the overweight. Colors that are bright, light, or serene might be just the thing you need to uplift a body you thought you'd rather hide. In fact, really dark colors, and black, can actually add the illusion of weight when they cover the body. As an overall visual impact, that dark color takes on pounds of its own in contrast to medium-and light-toned skin. Too much of a good, dark thing can create a blob effect. Look at it this way: a black swim-suit will actually make pale thighs appear heavier because of the contrast.

Basically, colors fall into two groups—cool colors and warm—though your eye can pick up thousands of color tones.

Cool colors are blue- and green-dominated, such as blue-purple, greenish- or bluish-beige or gray, and bluish- or greenish-brown. Warm colors are red-and yellow-dominated, such as red-brown, red-purple, reddish- or yellowish-beige and gray.

Some basic color guidelines for dressing thin:

▶ Cool (and dark) colors don't create shadows out-lining the body's bulges; they decrease height and should be used wherever you're heavy. They de-emphasize.

▶ Warm (and light or bright) colors do cause shadow outlines from the body; they increase height and should be used wherever you're thin. They emphasize.

▶ Also consider the psychology of the colors you wear. Think of your favorite heroine and how she's dressed: red suggests passion and aggression; yellow, cheeriness and a sympathetic nature; green, love of control and ego; lavender, refinement. And black, bless its eternal heart, signals as much stubbornness as sophistication.

▶ Try to build your basic wardrobe on one color, preferably black, navy, gray, or beige, which you supplement with contrasting colors as accent pieces. Definitely use eye-catching colors around your neck and face for emphasis.

▶ If you don't know which colors work best with your skin type, consult experts. (Clue: pale complexions get washed out in beige, blonde, and off-white; and orange can muddy olive skin.)

Shape

This is the most basic element of clothing, and understanding it will help you grasp the concept of proportion, which is essential to any well-dressed person — and vital for knowing how to slenderize with clothing.

Think, for a moment, like a designer:

"Here's this fabric, and here's this image I have for something sexy, classic, or revolutionary. How do I begin?

"I begin with the color, pattern (or lack of it), and texture of the fabric. I then put it into basic shapes."

Some basic design shapes include:
> Square (box)
> Elongated square (rectangle)
> Drape (horizontal folds)
> Gathers (rounded shapes)
> Triangle (wide base)
> Inverted triangle (wide top)
> Tunic (long rectangle)
> Tube (long egg shape)
> Balloon (all-around shape)
> Tent (overall triangle)
> Taper (rounded, inverted triangle)

If you can now visualize these basic shapes as outlines, you can already begin to see that if your body is bottom-heavy (a triangle), you don't put another triangle shape on top of it. A top-heavy woman wearing Austrian-shade drapes across her chest doubles her size. Gathered skirts blow up wide hips and waists, and a tent is definitely not for everybody.

Proportion

Although its secret is the relationships of various shapes, the easiest way to think of proportion is as "lengths and breadths."

You may have read in a major fashion magazine that "proportion is the key." Or maybe a salesperson (a bright one) has said, "I like the color on you, but the proportion is all wrong."

And you, with good reason, probably scratched your head.

Proportion is a subtle concept, and I think the reason most women are confounded by it is that they don't look at themselves in a full-length mirror. It's only when you look at yourself from head to toe, when you distance yourself to take all of you in, that you begin to get a glimmer that a bolero jacket above legs that are four-and-a-half feet long doesn't work, or that a skirt with a flounce at the hem will make short legs look even shorter.

When you use proportion properly, all those different shapes and lines in clothing and accessories will create one total, integrated, smooth, head-to-toe visual impact.

Imagine a woman walking down the street in front of you: she's about 5'6" tall and a bit heavy in the hips. She's wearing a charcoal tweed blazer, straight navy skirt, and cordovan leather boots that end about three inches below her hemline.

The first thing your eye records in this total vertical image is that glaring horizontal strip of flesh interrupting the dark vertical line from her skirt to her feet. If you've really mastered the art of looking from head to toe, you also would notice that her legs are a little short for her body, which means that strip of horizontal flesh only shortens her legs more because it cuts the vertical line.

Another example of optical illusion created by lines: a double-breasted jacket, because of its two vertical rows of buttons, is a perfect slenderizer for a thick torso.

With the information you gathered about your one-and-only body and these four fashion principles, you now have a working guide to developing a new fashion identity—a thinner one!

From this day forward, all you have to do is to look more closely at your own body in a full-length mirror, look more closely at which colors look best on you, study which patterns and textures in fabric work for you, and then swear you'll look in that full-length mirror, while you're nude, at least once a week (or once a month, if that's easier), and three times a day while you're dressed, preferably in different outfits.

Just stand there, nude, and re-evaluate your real body again and again. Then stand there, dressed, and figure out what the lines of the clothes are doing to (or for) your body. Even if you don nothing but an elastic-waist nightgown, a terry robe on top of pedal-pushers, or a shirt tucked into jeans, you're learning the art of proportion.

Congratulations—you've just learned the art of taking off five to 20 pounds without swallowing a single pill!

3 What's Best for Your Body

The next step in dressing thin is to take what you know about your body and the four basic fashion principles, and make that knowledge work for your own body.

Here's a brief sampling of which kinds of fashions, colors, shapes, proportions, and textures work best with the four basic body types.

Straight Up and Down

This is the only body that can get away with horizontal stripes (moderate ones), preferably in a long, thin chemise. Her round-all-over counterpart, however, should avoid any pattern that's horizontal and should incinerate clothes with set-in waists, dolman sleeves, and high necks.

A woman with a thick torso does best with anything that draws attention away from her thick midriff; no bright or wide belts for her.

This thick-waisted person (and also the short-waisted type) should emphasize her shoulders and neck to keep the eye from focusing on the midriff; a dress, sweater, or blouse with some scattered pattern or trim around the shoulders is a good choice. If this same person is busty, however, she should make sure the pattern is on the shoulders, not the chest.

A chemise in a dark color or in a dark pattern no larger than, say, a dandelion blossom, is an excellent choice for the straight-up-and-down body. It keeps the eye moving vertically, and since the coloration is dark, it helps thickness recede. For the round-all-over type, a dress in a float shape or one that has an empire waist is preferable because it doesn't accentuate her round outlines, as a linear chemise would.

Top-heavy

This body is usually busty, but not necessarily. (This is the body whose hips and thighs appear narrower than bust and shoulders; imagine an inverted triangle.)

Chances are, this woman doesn't need padding at the shoulders. Nor does she need extra emphasis of her bust and chest.

To maximize the good, this woman is best suited for dark tops and light bottoms, empire waists, open V-neck blouses. She's least suited for dolman sleeves, fuzzy sweaters and jackets, tight sweaters, and blouson or belted tops that add puffiness where it isn't needed.

Usually, this woman also has great, slender hips and legs, so she should show them for all they're worth. If, however, her legs used to be great but are now sporting behind-the-knee pads, skirts should definitely be calf-length, not knee-length; and for heaven's sake, make sure boots leave no skin showing beneath the skirt.

For this body type, the emphasis should be in a vertical line that either lifts the eye up with accent emphasis, such as big earrings, or pulls the eye down to those outstanding, narrow hips and legs. Emphasizing both of these areas without breaking the vertical line of the eye is optimum.

Turtlenecks, high-buttoned blouses, and blouses with tight closed-neck details only emphasize top heaviness. Thin coats with narrow raglan shoulders or narrow, set-in sleeves and with open necklines, however, work beautifully.

Bottom-heavy

It's said that 65% of American women look like triangles (though it's not said quite that way). These are the women who are heavier in the beam than in the shoulders and chest. They're inclined to have a short and/or thick waist; and I, for one, am delighted to learn that all those women whom I keep thinking look better than I do are only one-third of the female population.

By now, you already know that this is the body that needs dark colors at bottom, and light or bright colors and patterns on top. This woman really needs those flight-deck shoulders—anything at the shoulder line to bring out the shoulders and bring in the hips and thighs.

It is no accident that almost every woman on TV's "Dynasty," thanks to designer Nolan Miller, walks around with shoulders as big as her bed. Actresses of the thirties and forties knew the same trick; think of Joan Crawford.

Gathered skirts are disastrous for this woman. Jackets that hit mid-hip are just as horrible. Dresses with slightly dropped waists are winners, as are big tops and easy, classic trousers. Dark colors on top and light ones on the bottom are a horror. Big sleeves, but not weight-producing dolman ones, as well as brightly colored scarves and jewelry, go a long way to pulling the eye up to where the body is good and not down, to where it isn't.

Hourglass

Blessed with an indented waist, whatever the proportions above and below it, this is the woman who can daily curtsey to the continuing ideal of Victorian beauty. She's voluptuous, no doubt about it, and emphasizing that small waist is her trump card. I've seen my daughter shine in her well-wrapped waist since she was a teenager.

Romance looks just right on this woman. Padded shoulders and nipped waists are perfect partners. Flowing fabrics, whether they're cut on the bias or draped in folds, are great accents. Soft colors, as well as soft fabrics, enhance this romantic body.

This is the woman who can wear dresses that are fitted, traditional ones or in princess styles. Of the lot, she's the only body type who can.

Conversely, this is the woman who should ditch clingy tops and bottoms. She's also the woman on whom a tent dress is the worst choice unless she wants to look as if she's the shelter, not the woman, awaiting the sultan.

Other taboos: Boxy coats and jackets only turn her into a square, obtrusive shape, and fussy necklines and high necks give too much emphasis to her rounded top. Because she is so voluptuous, she should generally avoid earthy tones, shetland wools and anything else that has the businessman's hard, preppy edge. Chemises are equally adverse to her body type.

Soft is what she is, and soft is how she ought to appear. But remember, the emphasis here is on those curvaceous lines. As soon as she adds patch pockets

to her chest or stomach, she has ruined her natural
assets. The rule, then, is soft—in fabric, silhouette,
and coloration.

Hopefully, it's all beginning to make some sense.
You now have some pretty good notions of how to
apply the fashion principles of pattern, color, shape,
and proportion to your specific body type and wind
up looking thinner without having bought anything
more expensive than a blouse or belt.

But if you're becoming overwhelmed as you think,
"But my body's got other specific trouble spots," rest
easy. We'll talk about that next.

For now, just keep looking in that mirror, learning
all the nooks and crannies of your natural body and
all the tricks that line and color can do to make you
look thinner in the flash of anybody's eye.

4 Trouble Spots

Whatever your particular body configuration, it's yours. Never forget that. The same specifics of your body that annoy you are overshadowed by the things in your body that make you unique and wonderful.

Just remember that somewhere in that body of yours—from your head to your toes—there are features worth bragging about, and definitely worth maximizing.

Review the pluses and minuses of your body on your index card. Then, study this thumbnail sketch of clothing that works and doesn't work for specific trouble spots. You can avoid studying spots that don't apply to you, but you'll be better off if you study all of them, because you'll learn principles of proportion, pattern, and color until they really sink in.

These are the specific problems that cause the most worry—with suggestions for minimizing them.

Face and Neck

Big helps for fleshy faces are short hairstyles that come forward to frame the face, making it appear smaller, and makeup that contours fleshy areas. We'll discuss hair and makeup in Chapter 6.

As for fashion, big, important earrings, especially in slenderizing geometric shapes such as triangles, help "pull away" fleshy or round cheeks. Hats with low, big brims do the same (unless you have a short neck; then you'll look swatted).

Taboos for double chins are any collar styles that are ruffled, too large, too fluted, or too high, because they draw too much attention to your chin area.

▶ *Fleshy neck*—Tying a long, lightweight scarf in a low fold at the chest is one way to disguise thickness here. Chokers, but not oversized, bulky ones, are good neck accessories. Better are long ropes of beads or chains because they elongate.

What you do not want is any extra weight at your neck: ruffled collars, large, exaggerated collars, and thick, bulky scarves only add thickness. Boatnecks, turtlenecks, and stand-up collars only draw more attention to your face. Opt for open V-neck blouses and jackets or scoop-neck tops. That area of skin showing helps pull the eye to the face and elongate the upper body.

Back, Arms, and Shoulders

If your back is fleshy, avoid back-baring tops and evening dresses; strapless dresses will only pull your back into bulges. Thin chiffon or silk tops are good disguises, as are dark colors.

For fleshy arms, sleeve styles are the key to looking thinner. Avoid sleeveless clothes and sleeves that are short or fully gathered at the shoulder as well as leg-of-mutton sleeves and those cut full or billowy. Raglan and dolman sleeves also add bulk where you don't want it. Dropped-shoulder styles aren't good choices, either, because they pull the eye to the area where you want less, not more, attention. And never wear sweaters or knit tops with tight or bulky sleeves.

Better choices are long, slim-cut sleeves like those in a classic V-neck shirt. Shorter sleeves that do work are those that are narrowly (but not tightly) cut and which reach just above the elbow or two or three inches higher. Scoop necks, V-necks, and placket-closure polo styles also are good tops. The point is to keep the sleeves thin in appearance, with no gathers or extra puffiness.

▶ *Narrow shoulders*—The object here is to widen the appearance of your shoulders to balance the width of your hips and thighs. Obviously, in jackets, coats, and dresses, extended, well-padded shoulders are instant solutions. When it comes to tops and sweaters, you want to create the same wide illusion at the shoulders. Patterns such as horizontal stripes or tucks help.

Provided you don't have a fleshy neck, heavy arms, or double chin, wide cowl or draped necks will add width gracefully. Light colors will do the same. Fully cut sleeves, puffed or fluted ones, and wide dropped-shoulder styles also help—just make sure that the shoulder line isn't too tight or too close to your own shoulder line. Halter tops add width, too.

Big, flashy earrings, hair ornaments, and turban-tied scarves also help pull the eye to the face and away from narrow shoulders.

Bust

Have you ever seen a large-breasted woman in a clinging sweater or top? That may be OK for Dolly Parton types who want to emphasize their fullness, but if you want to de-emphasize fullness here, avoid clingy tops, strapless ones, low, draped necklines—any upper-torso style that maximizes, not minimizes, the extra.

Dolman sleeves only add fullness, as do sleeves that are cut too full. Ruffly necklines, halter tops, and high collars put the wrong kind of emphasis on the top-heavy woman, and horizontal patterns should be absolutely forbidden. Top styles that do work are V necks, scoop necks, narrow sleeves, and blouses with narrow stock ties or bows.

▶ *Small breasts*—Using the maximize-the-good formula, directing more attention to your upper torso is what you want in order to balance a wider torso below. (Remember, 65% of American women are wider in their hips and thighs than in their upper torsos, so the small-breasted woman is likely to belong in this category. These same guidelines, however, apply to a small-breasted woman who might be straight up and down.)

Good solutions are short, wide sleeves, and fully cut or gathered sleeves. Bright colors, elaborately beaded evening tops, and bold patterns in tops add the illusion of fullness. Horizontal stripes are another good choice. Clingy tops and sweaters, however, narrow the upper torso, and if they're too clingy, they also widen the appearance of the hips by contrast. The illusion you want to create is extra fullness in the chest.

Waist

Boy, do you want to de-emphasize a thick waist, given America's love of the baby-doll-waisted woman (think of the song about "The Girl that I Marry," who is also the "doll I can carry"). Here, you'll just have to accept what you do have and let myths fall where they may. Wearing a Scarlett O'Hara corset every day isn't the answer; fortunately, there are other fashion tricks in your favor.

A fitted waist is not one of them. Nor are clingy sweaters and tops, or those with heavy textures and patterns. Nor are light-colored dresses, unless they're chemises, empire, or tank styles. If both the top and bottom of an outfit are light-colored, make sure the jacket, tunic, or overblouse is long enough to cover the waist as well as a fitted waistband, if that's your choice for skirts or trousers.

What *will* help are vertical (not horizontal) stripes, those easy-fitting, thigh-length jackets and tops, skirts with dropped waists, and open vests that are longer than your waistline. Straight-legged trousers are infinitely better than tapered ones, and blouses or sweaters that blouse slightly above the waist are good choices (provided the skirt below is a straight or slightly flared style, or the trousers are cut straight). Select blouses and jackets with open necklines because they divert the eye upward.

Throw out harem pants and tapered skirts. Don't buy any dress or top that's accented with ruffles, buttons, or pattern in the midriff; tight waistbands and belts only draw more attention to this trouble spot. Bulky, quilted, and belted coats, and coats made of fur, do the same thing.

Select dresses with shoulder or neck accents to lift the eye. Chemises, caftans, empire, and dropped-waist dresses are wonderful waist disguises; ditto for darker colors and dresses with small patterns.

▶ *Short waist/long legs*—Unfortunately, short waists often accompany thick waists, so apply all the principles listed above for thick waists.

If your waist is higher in back than in front, you might as well throw away all your belts, unless you wear them under jackets. If you've ever spent a whole day trying to pull down your belt in the back, you know what an annoyance it is to feel your belt riding above your waistband and worry about how it looks.

Since short waists also usually accompany long legs, restudy those fashion principles above for skirts and pants. A quick reminder: straight, narrow, or flared skirts (below the knee or calf) and those with dropped waists keep proportion in balance. Classic straight-legged trousers are better than harem or blouson versions; wear them with the tops recommended above to balance your short/long proportions. Remember, too, that waist-length jackets are wrong, particularly fitted ones, because they make your waist appear even shorter and your legs longer.

▶ *Long waist/short legs*—Oh, you may think those long-waisted lovelies out there are the lucky ones; at least they don't look "choppy," you think. Well, truth is, they don't, but the other truth is that those long waists almost always come with short legs. Nature does have a way of tossing in the trouble with the glory.

The principle of balancing the body's proportions is again the goal. This woman just reverses the principles for short waists/long legs when mixing tops and bottoms.

For instance, waist-length or bolero-length jackets help camouflage extra waist length; so do jackets that are hip-length. But none of these jackets will work with skirts, such as flounced or ruffled ones, which just pull more attention to short legs and make them appear shorter. Slim, straight skirts that hit below the knee are best (unless you have thick lower legs, which you'll also have to camouflage). Trousers shouldn't emphasize short-leggedness, so stay away from pedal-pushers, cuffed trousers, elasticized ankles, and any bold detail on trousers such as patch pockets or contrasting trim.

Light, bright colors are good choices for tops, and dark colors that help lengthen the torso's vertical line are good for skirts and trousers. Very good are tops and bottoms in the same color value, because again, you don't want to chop the body's proportions with too much color contrast, unless the bottom color is one that elongates the legs.

Sweaters and tops with shoulder and neck accents pull the eye upward and away from your long waist/short legs proportions. Even short, waist-length sweaters work, provided they're worn with straight, elongating shapes in pants and skirts.

By all means, avoid vertical striping on tops and dresses. Be careful of sleeves that are too blousy, over-sized collars, and yoke details on tops. They bring the eye up, yes, but if these accents are too bulky or obvious, they overpower short legs, making them look shorter. Sweaters and jackets that hit at the thighs only shorten your legs more; so do long skirts or flounced ones.

Choose coats with vertical lines. Vertically worked furs, quilted styles, and straight, unbelted silhouettes, especially with extra neck and shoulder emphasis, lengthen legs and balance proportions. As in skirts, avoid lengths that are lower than just below the calf.

In dresses, the same principles for short waist/long legs types work, because the object is to disguise mis-matched lengthwise proportions. Small patterns or dark tones in dresses work. Easy-fitting dresses and chemises, and those with neck accents such as open necks and high collar emphasis, also work.

Believe it or not, belts don't work unless they're

contoured, hip-riding styles. But do believe that high heels are instant leg lengtheners; just make sure they're not so high that they throw off your balance and put you in a tilt position, because a non-erect posture will add pounds to anyone.

Tummy

Anything that draws attention to a well-padded tummy is to be avoided. The quickest way to make sure your techniques are working is to sidle up to that full-length mirror and look at yourself sideways again and again.

Tight-belted skirts or dresses will instantly pull in the area above the tummy, which pushes out the tummy even more. Better than tucked-in blouses in tight waistbands are tunics and overblouses, which help fill out the tummy bulge in symmetrical lines. Dresses in empire styles and those with dropped-waist blouson tops are excellent masquerades. Slightly flared tent styles and A-shaped silhouettes also work.

Gathered skirts and accordion pleats only add pounds. Better are fitted yoke skirts, stitched-down pleated styles, sarongs, wrap skirts, and A-line shapes. You can totally forget geometric patterns such as horizontal stripes, bulky weaves, and large plaids.

Short blouson jackets with fitted waists only draw attention to the tummy below. So do belted jackets, especially those with peplums. Hip-length vests and jackets, as well as sweater sets, cut away the appearance of tummy bulge. Even hip-length or waist-length sweaters that blouse above the waist will help balance the tummy's own blousiness.

Well-padded shoulders are great diverters, as are shoulder accents on dresses, blouses, sweaters, and jackets; for example, epaulets and flower motifs instantly pull the eye away from the trouble area.

Avoid, at all costs, clingy knits for skirts, dresses, and trousers, as well as big patch pockets or other accents in the stomach area. Classic, straight-leg trousers (*never* too tight) are right, provided they don't have too many pleats below the waistband. Blousy harem-style pants are wrong. Darker-colored bottoms—in the right silhouettes—are always right.

Derriere

Many of the same rules for the protruding tummy work for the protruding derriere, because often the two come together. Just keep looking at yourself sideways; you'll get the picture.

For heaven's sake, throw out any bottoms made from clingy fabrics and any tight panties that leave a discernible line around the thing you're trying to disguise.

Tight pants, shorts, and skirts are the first visions you want to abolish. So are those elaborately stitched accents, pockets, or patches on bottoms that pull the eye to the behind you wish you had already left. Cute little belts do the same. Shoulder bags that hit at hip level draw attention to this trouble spot. Good cover-ups for the beach are sarongs, not shorts.

Use the minimize principle for color: don't wear dark tops over light bottoms; reverse the combination. Jackets should hit just below the fullest width of your hips, not above, or you just bring extra attention to this protrusion.

Tunics are wonderful disguises, provided they're cut fully enough so they don't pull at your backside's fullness, accenting it even more. Jackets should be loosely fitted, too.

In dresses, lightly fitted styles work, but only if the skirt is a full A-line or bias cut. Belted styles in dresses and coats attract too much attention to what's below. Chemise dresses are good, but only if they're loose-fitting. Empire and A-line silhouettes also work.

Forget any big patterns below the waist, but do opt for shoulder and neck details and accessories to divert the eye upward.

▶ *No derriere*—If you've got other trouble spots covered, don't worry about this one. You can, of course, wear bold patterns and light, bright colors from the waist down as long as your body isn't mismatched with wide hips or saddlebags. (Almost always, it won't be, because a plywood backside usually comes with a top-heavy body type, which means gathered skirts are perfectly fine, and even thigh-exposing swimsuits, including those with bold patterns at the bottoms.) You also can get away with clingy bottoms. Bless your heart.

Thighs and Legs

Often, those extra pounds of flesh riding just below the hip line accumulate on the woman who is already full in the hips. If you have these bulges, it just means you have to be extra-careful that the fit of any bottom is looser and more flared through the thigh and hip area. Tapered bottoms will not work because they'll just outline those double curves.

Review the recommendations above for protruding tummy and protruding derriere. Again, the object is to minimize the extra, so if you keep the eye moving upward and if you select silhouettes, colors, and patterns that slenderize your bottom half, you've got your saddlebags under wraps.

▶ *Heavy lower legs and ankles*—Please don't flash them. Instant slenderizers are dark-toned hosiery and stockings with narrow vertical stripes. Remember, however, that contrast hosiery—that is, hosiery darker than the skirt above it—will cut the visual line from the waist down. Maintaining a single color tone in skirt and hosiery is a good rule for all body types.

With thick ankles and lower legs, you certainly don't want to wear pedal-pushers or knee-length Bermudas that will immediately draw the eye to the lower leg.

High heels help slenderize, as do sling-back pumps, but sandal-style heels and dizzy colors and patterns in shoes only call attention to these trouble spots. So will ankle socks and ankle jewelry. Flats aren't a good idea, unless they're very subdued in style and color and they're worn with trousers or with skirts and hosiery in dark coordinating colors.

Do you feel better about your body now? You should, now that you've learned that your body has a lot of pluses—more pluses than minuses.

By now, you've also gotten a good working knowledge of the slenderizing techniques that will work for you. (By the way, they'll work for you even if you lose a little weight.)

Jot down what you've learned about your trouble spots on your personal index card (or a new one), so that it becomes an instant checklist of your body type, including any specific trouble spots you want to de-emphasize.

Keep that recorded information about yourself with you—plus your personal insights about colors and workable styles that make you feel good about yourself—whenever you go shopping.

The six things you should know when you go shopping are these:

▶ What is my body type?
▶ Where do I gain the most weight?

▶ What are my best assets?
▶ What colors make me feel happy?
▶ What's the occasion I'm shopping for?
▶ Which new clothes will work with ones I already have and still be OK if I lose some weight?

So, you now know who you are—specifically what your body is all about—and, knowing that, what you should look for (and look out for) before you say yes to anything at the store.

No impulse shopping, please!

It doesn't matter how much you like that flower-splattered gathered skirt. If you've got wide hips, a short waist, or a protruding tummy, forget it. Go dark and sleek, not billowy and bright.

You'll look thinner, and you'll be happier—and that, after all, is what looking thin and feeling beautiful are all about.

Another round of applause to you.

We'll now look at everything you know about your body and apply it to specific kinds of dressing.

Just keep going and breathe a sigh of relief; the best is yet to come.

5 Your New Fashion Identity

Using the battery of information you have about yourself, now we'll look at specific kinds of dressing and find out how your body is best dressed for any occasion.

Take the recommendations you'll see here, then apply them to what you already know about your body and the fashion principles of pattern, color, shape, and proportion.

It's easier than it may sound.

Business Looks

Don't think a dark pinstriped suit and floppy bow tie are the only solution for serious negotiations. Yes, that dark pinstriped or flannel suit will work for all body types, but there are some fashionable, slenderizing accents you can add to it. There are even slimming alternatives to the business suit.

Stylish, slimming accents to serious looks include V-neck blouses and scoop-neck blouses for all body types. A dark Chanel bow in the hair also brings attention to the face and away from trouble areas.

Broad-shouldered jackets are great for the bottom-heavy woman; so are light jackets and darker skirts.

For office dressing, a good choice for the top-heavy woman is a pinstriped suit. This red-and-white pinstriped cotton suit with slightly fitted jacket and large V collar help minimize fullness on top, and the narrow set-in sleeves don't add more fullness. A large-brimmed white straw hat is set back on the head to avoid shortening the neck. These great slim legs look wonderful with pale stockings to continue the color line of the suit (but thick legs would need medium-toned stockings). Sling-back pumps are slenderizers for all body types.

For the top-heavy woman, reverse the contrast to dark tops and lighter bottoms. For that straight-up-and-down woman, dark-toned chemises are wonderful. The hourglass woman looks serious in a dark-colored, well-belted shirtwaist dress. And a Chanel-styled dress, or a Chanel suit with a straight skirt and contrasting trim on a hipbone-length jacket works for all body types.

The full-breasted woman can slenderize with a narrow stock-tie blouse. A fleshy neck and face look thinner with business accents such as long ropes of pearls or chains and important, but not outlandish, earrings. The woman with thick lower legs and ankles always looks right in dark skirts and dark hosiery.

The photographs here illustrate a slenderizing but fashionable look in a Chanel-style knit dress for the bottom-heavy woman and a plaid suit with a slightly nipped waist for the straight-up-and-down woman.

Businesslike dresses are never wrong for the office. If you're bottom-heavy, choose a light tone for top and a dark tone for those wide hips and thighs. This two-piece Chanel-styled dress is a perfect choice. Hips are slenderized by the black skirt. A collarless white top with black trim helps bring the eye up to the face. Add long ropes of necklaces and chains and large gold earrings, plus extra shoulder pads, to emphasize the top torso, which is narrow in the shoulders and needs lengthening and widening.

For a straight-up-and-down body, a body-shaping (but not tight) jacket and flared skirt give the illusion of shape. The pattern of the Glen Plaid suit is not too large, so it doesn't add thickness. The suit features a one-button closure jacket with padded shoulders and slightly fitted waist. A floral print stock-tie blouse and large round pin at the shoulder bring more attention to the face.

Shirts, Blouses, and Trousers

Whether worn for work or weekend life, these basics can take off lots of inches when chosen according to your body's specifications. All body types can get away with wearing trousers—if they have the right patterns, colors, and proportions.

Ruffly, high-necked blouses in bright colors would turn a top-heavy woman into a blimp, but could be a real boon to the long-waisted woman with an average neck and no top-heaviness. V-neck and scoop blouses

To accentuate her narrow hips and thighs, the top-heavy woman wears a light skirt. A dark blouse—one with slim, set-in sleeves, slender bow tie, and small pattern—works best. Long ropes of pearls add slimness to her top, and square, over-sized earrings balance her round, fleshy face and short neck.

work for all body types because that exposed area of skin at the neck lengthens the entire line of the body.

Sweaters don't have to add pounds, either. The bottom-heavy woman benefits from a bulky knit sweater with strong shoulder accents, though it would destroy the looks of her top-heavy sister. An hourglass woman can definitely benefit from a tight-waisted sweater provided it's not too hefty and its sleeves don't billow. Open sweater vests add length to the short-waisted woman, and hip-length sweaters work for everybody but the bottom-heavy woman.

Classic, straight-legged trousers are a blessing for all types. Women with great legs can wear pedal-pushers. Clingy narrow pants are just fine for top-heavy women blessed with narrower hips.

See how a dark, small-patterned blouse slenderizes a top-heavy woman and how easy-fitting, dark classic trousers narrow the beam of a bottom-heavy woman.

Classic, straight-legged trousers are a boon for the bottom-heavy woman. Equally important, to fill out her narrow upper torso, is a brightly colored blouse—one with pleats at bodice and shoulders, extra shoulder pads to widen her torso, and a jewel neckline to lengthen her short neck. With the wide top, hip proportions are solved. Add a bright, narrow leather belt to balance the entire vertical silhouette. Flat shoes and nude stockings keep the long vertical line uninterrupted.

Jackets

What would we do without them? They cover a multitude of sins, but if chosen in the wrong length, color, or pattern, they can make us look as if we've been on a three-month banana split binge.

Imagine a straight-up-and-down woman in a belted black and white plaid jacket with big patch pockets on the peplum. On second thought—don't! Now imagine the same woman in a wide-shouldered, tapered, hipbone-length jacket in a cream tint worn with a tapered, below-the-knee skirt in a soft pastel. Big difference!

Since jackets can be worn with dresses as easily as with slacks and skirts, they're a fashion necessity. But since their fabrics automatically add thickness, just make sure the wrong color, style, and length will not add even more.

A long, dark, below-the-hipbone jacket is a great slenderizer for the bottom-heavy woman. The pattern is small, the colors are dark, and the low, one-button V-neck closure helps to lengthen her short torso. Long ropes of necklaces and a blouse with a dropped jewel neckline also help to lengthen her short torso and extend her short neck. Large round earrings balance her angular features. A straight, medium-toned skirt is perfectly fine here because the jacket covers those wide hips and thighs.

In the photos here, note how a broad-shouldered, paisley jacket that comes below the top of the hip adds top width to balance the bottom-heavy woman. For the hourglass woman, a jacket with wide, geometric lapels worn with a scoop-necked tank top and fitted straight skirt shows off her curves.

The hourglass woman slenderizes with a soft yellow suit with straight skirt and large geometric-lapel jacket. The large, flat lapels help slenderize her top heaviness. Add a long necklace and scoop-neck top to slenderize and lengthen the upper torso. For the full face, add dangling "straight" earrings to de-emphasize fleshiness in the face.

Skirts

Most of us wear more skirts than trousers or dresses, and thank goodness we no longer have to wear man-tailored slacks to be taken seriously.

Given their popularity and versatility, and given your extra pounds, choose styles, lengths, and colors carefully. Whether chosen for boardroom meetings or black-tie evenings, the right skirt can not only slenderize, but entice.

For the hourglass woman, her best asset is her waist. Here it's emphasized with a three-inch wide red belt. The blouse, with fitted narrow sleeves, a small floral pattern and jewel neckline, doesn't add fullness; nor does the straight narrow skirt.

A long, sarong-wrapped skirt in black or navy crepe for evening wear is a treasure for the bottom-heavy woman. Conversely, a flounced peasant skirt style, whatever the fabric, is a disaster for the short-legged woman. Brightly colored gathers and pleats are just fine for that top-heavy type, and tight-waisted flared skirts look oh so grand on that hourglass woman. Anyone with tummy bulge or hippiness doesn't always have to opt for a straight, ungathered skirt in black or navy; skirts in lighter colors with stitched-down pleats or flattening yokes work just fine.

Remember that colors and patterns can intensify weight, in skirts as in everything else. A bold Glen plaid is certainly a disaster for everyone but that top-heavy woman, but small herringbones and gingham checks work for all body types, provided the silhouette and length are correct.

To illustrate, the photograph here shows how a tight-waisted skirt enhances the curves of an hourglass figure. The small-patterned blouse with narrow, set-in sleeves doesn't add bulk to her top, and a snug floral belt emphasizes her best features.

Dresses

Like skirts, these are instant feminizers, and femininity is no longer a bad word. The key to selecting the right dress for you is knowing every nook, cranny, and bulge of your body.

It's that hourglass woman who is enhanced, not ballooned, by a fitted dress, but chemises are safe for all body types, provided they don't come with a top or sleeve treatment that's wrong for your particular body.

Details to look for are accents in the right spots (such as patterns or epaulets on the shoulders for the

53

straight-up-and-down and bottom-heavy woman, or open necks for the top-heavy woman). Other accents are the locations of pockets and pleats and the length of the dress. All the little details—ruffles, buttons, contrast stitching, collar styles, and the cut of the sleeves—can amplify or enhance your body. Just please don't ever fall in love with a dress, then wonder why you never get any compliments when you wear it.

By the way, recording the compliments you do get—every time you get them—is a great tool to help you understand what colors and styles are working for you. It also will help you throw out any piece of clothing that leaves everyone mute.

Study the dresses here, and see how they work for different body types. By all means study the pattern, silhouette, length, and such accents as neck, shoulder, and arm treatments.

This two-piece dress features a dropped blouson top that fits across the hips and a long, fitted skirt with a godet hem. This gives shape to a straight-up-and-down body, but it also could work for a top-heavy woman, because the top isn't too blousy and the neckline isn't fussy. Narrowness through the hips and thighs contrasts with the fullness of the padded-shoulder top, giving more body shape. Hair is pulled up to widen the shoulders. High heels add length to the long skirt, and the floral pattern is not so large that it widens the body.

The bottom-heavy woman might have real problems wearing a dress with a gathered skirt or one whose skirt is too tight or too boldly patterned. *Because her shoulders are narrower than her hips, it's the shoulders she wants to emphasize.* Here, a V-neck, fitted halter dress with flared skirt is a perfect choice for warm weather. The halter top gives the illusion of more shoulders, and the flared skirt evens out her wide hips and thighs. Nor are the polka dots so large that they add more fullness.

The top-heavy woman wants to de-emphasize her bust with a dark color. A straight, light-colored skirt emphasizes her good qualities—narrow hips and thighs. This two-piece dress does just that. The padded shoulders and white V-shaped spread collar help bring the eye up to her face. Black pumps and light stockings show off her slender legs.

Even during office hours, there's nothing wrong with that hourglass woman showing her waist. Here, a brown leather belt accents her good feature. The dress with its V neck extends the vertical line of her curvaceous body. A large pin on the shoulder and large earrings also help bring the eye upward. Note, also, that the sleeves are not too billowy, which would only add weight to her full upper torso.

Coats and Furs

These are the big cover-ups, and, like jackets, they can add heaviness just by the sheer weight of their fabric. Details are critical here, because a coat, like a dress, creates one uninterrupted image.

Long-haired furs should be taboo for anyone carrying a bit more than her own fighting weight. Better choices are fur coats with the skins worked vertically. They'll elongate any body type, and they're excellent lengtheners for short-legged women.

In choosing any coat, check out the silhouette: a cape is a wonderful disguise for problems below the waist, but a belted coat, horizontal quilting, and even released pleats in the back of a coat can sabotage the images of bottom-heavy types.

Straight or slightly flared coats are good silhouettes for everybody, but the wrong details can ruin even those silhouettes. Big, full sleeves only add fullness to the top-heavy woman; belts ruin the thinner look for those women with derriere, hip, or waist thickness; trim on the bottom of the coat can cut inches off short

A classic, straight-lined coat assures an overall slimming silhouette that's good for any body type and is particularly effective for a bottom-heavy woman who can't risk belted or fitted styles. The wide, padded shoulders and high, slightly puffed sleeves and collar pull attention to the shoulders and add the illusion of balance, and the loose, straight cut adds length to her short legs. A high pillbox hat with a large pin as an extra accent pull the eye upward.

legs; obvious rows of buttons or closures can thicken, even more, thick-through-the-middle types.

In the straight silhouette coat shown here, you can see how wide shoulders add the illusion of balance to the bottom-heavy woman.

Evening Looks

Thank goodness for those black-tie evenings that give us a chance, in the prettiest ways, to disguise any extras at all. Because so many evening gowns are long, all body types look like winners in them, especially if they have narrow, fluid silhouettes.

Recall what you've already learned about maximizing the good and minimizing the extra. Proportion and details are critical, unless you think a long black gown and a rope of pearls is the only way to go.

Successes: elaborately beaded tops, padded or draped shoulder treatments, and gussied-up strapless tops for bottom-heavy women; halter or scoop-neck

An hourglass figure could wear a belted or waist-fitting evening gown, but for real impact, a long beaded sheath with a V neckline helps pull attention to the face and creates a long, fluid line. White is just fine in this case because the shape of the dress doesn't accentuate curves. An uplifted hairstyle and long dangling earrings add emphasis to the face.

tops for short or thick-waisted types; V necks and scoop necks in long chemise silhouettes for top-heavy types.

Misfires: low, open backs and strapless styles for the well endowed; handkerchief hems and flounced tea-length dresses for short-legged women; fitted, clingy silhouettes for bottom-heavy types; tight-waisted dresses around wide waistlines.

Be really careful about details, silhouettes, fabric, and color; a mistake in evening wear is extra-costly.

The evening dresses here illustrate how a black chemise with narrow arms works for a top-heavy woman, and how a wide-shouldered, beaded V-neck top works for the bottom-heavy woman.

You can't go wrong with a classic black sheath for black-tie events. This short knit chemise helps slenderize the top-heavy woman's upper torso. The shawl collar de-emphasizes her top heaviness. Note the boat neck of the dress, which helps lengthen a short neck. A black satin draped cloche helps slenderize the overall silhouette, and sheer black stockings and black high heels continue the long, dark, vertical line.

Come evening, the bottom-heavy woman should choose a hip-slenderizing ensemble, and a beaded two-piece dress solves many figure problems. The V neck adds length to a short torso, and an overblouse top disguises a thick waist. The narrow skirt brings no unwelcome attention to the hips, and the scalloped hemline dramatizes good legs. Metallic, high-heeled sandal pumps add even more length, and balance overall proportions.

Leisure and Active Wear

When it's time to kick off your shoes for some weekend or vacation fun, remember it's that same body trying to look right in a swimsuit, jumpsuit, short shorts, or clingy top. Less can definitely be too much in the case of these body-conscious clothes.

Obviously, you don't sidle into some short shorts if your thighs are wide; better choices are loosely fitted mid-thigh styles, but not in wide stripes or plaids or ones with pockets or other accents. Capri pants cut away short legs; clingy polo shirts turn other women into exploding diva types.

Jumpsuits are good for most types unless they have tight waists (those are for the hourglass woman) or too much pocket or flap detail in areas best ignored. Sarong skirts or body wraps are perfect cover-ups for most of us, and shoulder-baring tops bring whistles for everybody but those divas.

In swimwear, high-cut maillot styles flatter hippy and thigh-heavy women, but if you have pale skin, avoid black because of the stark contrast with your thighs. Choose small or striped patterns if your body is thick. If you're thin around the bust, put bold patterns or ruffles there, but if you're thick around the bottom, avoid emphasis there. Blouson tops help balance heavy hips and disguise short, thick waists.

Just remember those basic principles. The less skin you've got showing, the more chances you have of being dynamite on the beach, the tennis court, the cruise ship, and in your very own home.

The photographs here show how above-the-knee cuffed shorts are right for a top-heavy woman, how a V-necked jumpsuit and contoured hip belt give shape to a straight-up-and-down woman, and how a boldly patterned swimsuit flatters a bottom-heavy body.

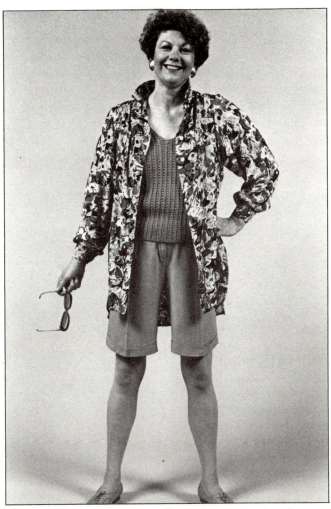

If you've got great legs, flaunt them. Khaki-colored walking shorts with cuffs show off great legs and narrow hips and thighs. A V-neck blouson sweater in a medium color helps slenderize top heaviness. A big, brightly-colored floral shirt adds extra dash, but no extra fullness. This same outfit works for a straight-up-and-down body, and would work for a bottom-heavy woman if the shorts were dark.

A black V-neck jumpsuit is a great choice for a straight-up-and-down body; it also would work for a top-heavy woman if it didn't have those dolman sleeves. A contour belt at the hips and extra shoulder pads give more body definition.

Patterns are important when choosing swimwear. If you need bust emphasis, choose bold patterns there; if you're bottom-heavy, big orchids and horizontal stripes won't work below. For a bottom-heavy woman with wide hips, thighs, and saddlebags, a pattern like this will work—a medium-sized one. A floating overskirt is a great solution for wide hips, thighs, and saddlebags. A scoop-neck top lengthens the upper torso and widens the shoulders; the suit's skirt hides a multitude of sins. The swimsuit's color, a light yellow which is close to this woman's naturally fair skin tone, helps create a unified look.

Lingerie

That "significant other" has probably already told you what works for you, and you can rely on someone else's responses, as well as your own feelings, to tell you what looks right in the night.

In nightgowns, some obvious mistakes are fitted waist styles for thick waists and overworked bodice treatments for those who already have ample bosoms.

A good all-round style is that long A-shape with an empire cut, which feminizes all body types.

Small-breasted, wide-hipped, short-waisted? No problem! For the bewitching hours, choose an empire-styled nightgown. Here, the A-line silhouette of the dark skirt disguises wide hips. The empire bodice with white trim adds more allure to the top. It's the perfect slenderizer for the bottom-heavy or straight-up-and-down woman.

For undergarments, choose hip-hugging bikinis (but not ones with narrow elastic bands) unless you're narrow-waisted or slim-hipped. If your thighs are larger than you like, choose loose-fitting tap pants. If you're full-busted, you don't want underwires or too tight a fit, both of which will give you bulges where you don't want them. If your body is thick, choose slips with slightly flared silhouettes.

In *all* lingerie, the cardinal rule is never to buy anything too tight. If your back and breasts are full, tight lingerie will cause bulges, and a tight slip will ride up into visible creases. Any panties that are too tight are guaranteed to be seen under shorts, trousers, or snug skirts, and those panty lines are the last thing you want showing, even if you're slim-hipped.

Accessories

Bless them, one and all. They're the least expensive way to dramatize any outfit, to add emphasis where you need it, to make your head-to-toe appearance look finished. Little things do mean a lot.

Whatever your shape, always draw attention to your face. Big, brightly colored earrings, as well as the right necklaces and brooches, do that, too.

Hats create mystery, so if you're round-faced, try one with a high crown, and if you don't have a short neck, choose a hat with a big brim and lower crown.

In bags, the classic shape is envelope, whether a clutch or shoulder bag: it's slimming, elegant, and never adds bulk. Conversely, an oversized saddlebag banging on your wide hips brings the eye straight to a trouble spot. Pouchy handbags do the same thing to any round area below the waist.

In footwear, shoes and hosiery should always be color-coordinated. If you want to lengthen your legs, choose dark tones; if you want to slim them, choose them again. Moderately high heels work for everybody, as do wedges. High heels certainly lengthen short legs, and oval-toed pumps and sling-back pumps slenderize every foot. Avoid any boots that aren't tall enough to be hidden by your skirt or trouser hem.

The two best accessories you have, you don't have to buy: always smile, and always stand erect. Both are instantaneous thinners. A frown drops your whole face, which then looks heavier, and a slumped-over body looks crumpled and at least ten pounds heavier.

A small, square shoulder bag adds no pounds. Equally important to a bottom-heavy woman is the skirt: a stitched-down yoke front with released pleats below the hipbone slenderizes wide hips, saddlebags, and protruding tummy.

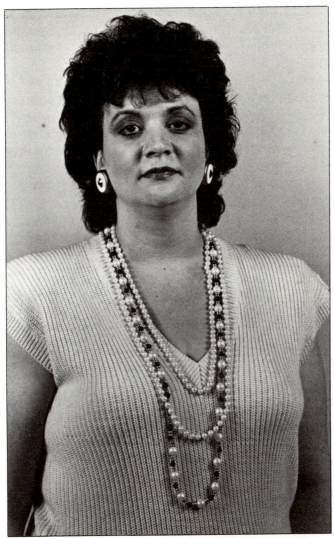

To *slenderize fullness on top*—whether you're a top-heavy woman or an hourglass shape—requires lengthening. A pastel, *V-neck sweater* accomplishes this, and *long necklaces* elongate a short, wide neck. *Large, round earrings* add even more facial emphasis.

When you wear boots, whatever your body type, make sure the hem of your skirt covers the top of the boots. A line of flesh between the two is an eyesore that breaks the vertical line and automatically adds more weight to your lower half.

Hats are a good finishing touch for any body type. A woman with a round, fleshy face and a short neck who adds a geometric-brimmed hat brings the eye up and away from her round face and lengthens her short neck. (If she were to wear a short-crowned, big-brimmed hat, she would look squashed.) The V-neck jacket lengthens her neck, too.

6 Makeup and Hairstyles

Now that you know how to dress your body, let's move up to your face and hair.

Your face is the first thing everybody notices, so smile! An engaging, happy face is one of your most flattering attributes: it entices others to look at your face, and it takes off inches and years; a frown pulls your entire face down and makes you look older, as well as less appealing.

Makeup

Learn the tricks of contouring and highlighting. This is what movie stars learn their first day on the set, and the same techniques that work for them will work for you.

The techniques are simple, according to Chris Welles, a New York hair and makeup artist who paints and combs stars almost daily. He puts the finishing touches on models for magazines such as *Vogue, L'Officiel, Mademoiselle,* and *Cosmopolitan,* and his private clients include film and TV stars as well as the Queen of Spain.

The basic rule of makeup artistry is contouring, or darkening, those areas of the face you want to recede

To flatter a round face, apply contouring under cheekbones and under the chin line. Here, extra eyeshadow is applied to the outside of the eyelids and extended to the end of the brow line. Eyebrows are darkened. Hair is pulled up and away from the face to dramatize it even more and to lengthen a short neck. A V-neck blouse further lengthens the neck, and a hair ribbon with a rhinestone pin and large, rectangular earrings flatter a round face.

and highlighting your beautiful features. (Come on now, we all have them.)

Contouring is using darker powders on fleshy or broad areas of the face. Welles suggests a soft, peachy tone for day and a browner, slightly darker powder for evening.

An example: "The best way to get rid of that double chin is to shade it in a darker powder from under the chin back to the line of the neck down to the Adam's apple," Welles suggests. "This will create a stronger or nicer jawline."

For a round, fleshy face, Welles says, "First of all, you have to find your cheekbone. Once you've discovered your cheekbone, use a highlighter (lighter-colored or glossy powder) on top of the bone; then, underneath the cheekbone, use a contouring powder. Finally, to soften the area where you've used highlighter and contouring, brush the entire area with a soft powder in your natural skin tone.

"If you have a beautiful pair of eyes, you don't have to use that much makeup to dramatize them. If they're close-set, only use dark shadows on the outside, not inside, of the lids."

But don't be afraid to add some extra shading to your eyelids and extra mascara to your lashes. Your eyes are the one feature you want to stand out. You really want to open those "windows" and invite everyone in; accented eyes are the best way to draw attention to your face.

A bit of extra coloring for lips and cheeks helps dramatize your face, too. You don't want to look like a kewpie doll, but you do want people to take notice of your face. In other words, you can never be "too bright," day or night, but you certainly want to use the brightest coloring only for night.

Welles suggests using a lighter shade of lipstick,

according to your skin tone, if your lips are full; if they're thin, you can be a little more dramatic with color and use a lip liner or pencil to outline them and make them appear more prominent. "But you don't want them to appear overpainted," Welles cautions.

If you're not sure of the best colors for your skin type, or where and how to color and contour your face, go to your favorite department store and find a cosmetic salesperson you trust. Shop around for the best expert. One good tip as to whether this person really knows her or his business is to ask for the right foundation for your skin type; if the "expert" applies it to the back of your hand, explain that the skin on your hand isn't the same as that on your face, and move on till you find a cosmetic specialist who knows this. That's the one you can trust.

Hair

Your hairstyle can add, or subtract, weight. One expert stylist, Monsieur Marc of New York, whose national following extends from Hollywood to the White House, points out that there's a right hairstyle for every woman.

The main thing to remember, says Marc, is that "hair is a frame to the face and a glory to the woman. The first thing a man will look at is your face and your hair. You can wear the most beautiful dress, and the wrong hair can ruin it. So you must communicate with your hairdresser, and above all, find the right length hairstyle for your face."

Specific recommendations:

For the round-faced or big-faced woman, "always bring the hair forward, because it makes the face appear smaller. A short, swept-back style brings the face forward and exposes it," Marc says. "If a woman has a full forehead, a few bangs help it to look smaller." (Didn't think proportion principles applied to your tresses?)

For those who are endowed with short, fleshy necks, Marc recommends against short hair "because it exposes your short neck. Keep your hair to a maximum of two or three inches longer than your chin line."

Double chin? The right hairstyle can slenderize that,

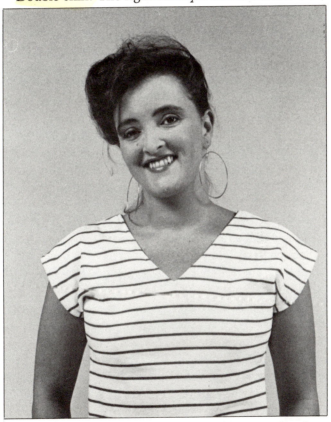

To soften a rectangular face, hair is pulled up and to the side and given fullness on top. The style allows this woman's dark, soulful eyes to shine.

too. "You can never wear hair shorter than your chin-line profile," Marc explains. Keep the profile of the style lower than the chin.

A profile and a back view are mandatory for choosing the right hairstyle—these are the views that tell you the truth, Marc says. "I recommend a three-way mirror. Everybody looks good from the front, but a profile view will show you what you don't want to see." This view will show you whether a style is too flat on top for your head, or not full enough from the back, for example.

These back and side views of your hairstyle also will tell you whether its fullness is appropriate for your overall body shape. Here, you want *full-length* side, front, and back views of yourself. A super-short, close-to-the-head style is not appropriate for any body type with extra pounds. It makes your head look smaller and your body bigger. Super-full styles won't work, either, certainly not for round-all-over and top-heavy types; they just add the illusion of more fullness to your body.

Another hairstyle rule to remember, according to Marc, is that shorter styles work for every woman. "Short hair makes you look younger," he says. As for the myth about long hair being sexy, Marc concedes that most men do think it's sexy, but adds that "long hair isn't necessarily sexy." Proportion is the key, he points out; "you can't have a little head on a big body. Lots of hair on a thin body makes more sense."

Accentuating your hair with color is another slenderizer. It brings extra attention to your face and makes you look younger. The color of your eyes determines the color your hair should be, Marc suggests; for example, if you have brown eyes, use a reddish-brown or chestnut hair color. With blue or green eyes, you can go either blonder or darker, but even blondes should never take the platinum Boardwalk route. A safe guideline is to choose a color that's one or two shades lighter or darker than your natural color.

To draw even more attention to your face, Marc recommends hair ornaments, scarves, bows, and combs—tortoise-shell and other dark combs for day, and ones with sparkly stones for evening. Bows and scarves tied as turbans add yet another accent.

A face with chiseled features and no real double chin benefits from a hairstyle that's brushed to the side, which opens up these naturally pretty features and appears to lengthen the neckline.

7 A New You

Now you've learned how to discover the real you, how to masquerade it where you will, and how to feel better about yourself—because now you know that your body's not nearly so imperfect as you might have thought.

You've also learned that basic fashion principles, which even superstar bodies use to maximize the good, are at your instant disposal. You've discovered, too, that a smile combined with a proud, erect bearing is an automatic slenderizer.

You also may have realized that you like those extra pounds just fine, thank you, and that if you still want to look a bit slimmer, that's perfectly fine, too.

Most of all, I hope you've come to know that you're beautiful, and that pounds have nothing to do with love.

I hope you feel thinner already—I know you know how to dress that way!

Four Basic Solutions

Left: *A straight-up-and-down woman can create contours by wearing a V-neck, blouson sweater and flared skirt. An upswept hairstyle and bold necklace add emphasis to her face.*

Second from left: *A top-heavy woman needs to maximize her hips, and a light skirt with stitched-down pleats lets her narrow hips show. A black, V-necked blouse and long ropes of pearls minimize her top-heavy proportions.*

Second from right: *Wide hips are no problem, even in a pastel-colored dress (yes, even a soft pink!) as long as the skirt is flared, not pleated. Shoulder pads and glittery, multicolored chokers add shape and sparkle and help balance bottom-heavy proportions.*

Right: *Bless her curvaceous heart! A woman with an hour-glass figure can carry an ensemble as bold as this fuscia, cowl-necked top worn with a jade-green sarong skirt and tied up with a pretty floral tapestry belt.*